The Freedom of the Press

THE
GRANADA
GUILDHALL LECTURES
1974

THE FREEDOM
OF THE PRESS

THE HALF-FREE PRESS
by Harold Evans

GOVERNMENT AND THE MEDIA
by Lord Windlesham

THE FREEDOM OF THE AMERICAN PRESS
by Katharine Graham

with an
Introduction by the Chairman,
Sir William Haley

Hart-Davis, MacGibbon   London

Granada Publishing Limited
First published in Great Britain 1974
by Hart-Davis, MacGibbon Ltd
Frogmore, St Albans, Hertfordshire, AL2 2NF and
3 Upper James Street, London W1R 4BP

Copyright © 1974 by Granada

ISBN 0 246 10827 4

Printed in Great Britain by
Cox & Wyman Ltd,
London, Reading and Fakenham

CONTENTS

PREFACE

THE Granada Guildhall Lectures on the theme 'Communication in the Modern World' began in 1959. They have covered the whole spectrum of arts, sciences, politics and mass media. Each lecturer, while concerning himself with communication in its broadest context, has dealt in particular with the practical implications of his subject for the world of today and tomorrow.

The lecturers in this series – distinguished scholars, writers and administrators – have been drawn from all walks of life and from all over the world. They have each set the standards for what Granada considers one of the most important and constructive series of lectures in the field of communications.

INTRODUCTION FOR THE BOOK
by the Chairman
SIR WILLIAM HALEY

THIS year's Granada Guildhall Lectures have many merits. Two are paramount.

The speakers had all had practical experience in dealing with the problems they were discussing. Mr Harold Evans had earned the reputation of being the most courageous editor in Britain today by his undaunted fight on behalf of the thalidomide victims, and his efforts to probe the origins of the tragedy. Lord Windlesham was Lord Privy Seal in Mr Heath's government when it resigned and had overall responsibility for all Government information. Mrs Katharine Graham pioneered investigatory journalism in *The Washington Post*; its long and inexorable uncovering of so many facets of the Watergate scandal made it for a time the most quoted newspaper in the world. Between them they could describe at first hand the pressures – what Lord Windlesham averred were the necessary and two-way pressures – between Authority and the Press.

The other outstanding merit of the Lectures was their timeliness. The issues involved in the freedom of the Press (an omnibus word that in this connection includes Television, Radio, and all means of communication by publication) are not academic. They are real, and immediate. It is the hard-headed people, not merely the alarmists, who are saying that the grave economic hazards we face may bring political and social perils in their wake. If the crisis does deepen, the strain on journalists and broadcasters will be intense. The open pressures on their freedom may be great. The hidden pressures will be even greater. The graver the situation becomes, the more persuasively will they be told that to reveal the whole truth would be dangerous, that the outlook is too precarious for *complete* candour.

In such circumstances the Press and Broadcasting will need to be clear-minded and resolute. They must assent to no such propositions. There is no pass to which affairs can come, when knowledge will not be better than fear of the unknown; information safer than ignorance. It will be said that the public is not politically educated enough to stand such shocks. There can be no education by suppression. And no shock to a nation is so great as for it to lose confidence in those it has trusted to keep it informed. If freedom is essential to truth, truth is equally essential to freedom.

Mr Evans's contrast between the long-accepted freedom of opinion and the still contested freedom of facts, particularly by the Law, is important. The fight for the freedom of facts, the freedom to disclose facts, is now at the heart of the matter. (It is worth recalling that in the February General Election some opinions became facts and Authority hankered after stifling them.)

Many people see the freedom of the Press as a contest between the editors and authority, with the ring held by the Law. They are prepared to accept this. To the extent that it is true, it is unsatisfactory. For the Law to be the ultimate arbiter of what we can and cannot know is a frail safeguard. Lawyers are by nature restrictive. The Law is in essence a mediaeval institution with mediaeval ideas of closed associations. There are individual Judges who are good. But the Law as a whole inhibits.

A third contestant needs to be added – public opinion. Thinking of Watergate and imagining its happening in Britain, I have more than once asked myself, leaving on one side whatever formal restrictions there might have been, whether the editors would have persisted. Would they have devoted the man-power, the money, the space, and the time – not days and weeks, but months and years – as *The Washington Post* did? Or would they have been afraid of the reactions of their readers, ranging from boredom to downright hostility? The Press needs freedom from its readers as much as it does from constituted authority. The more intolerant a paper's readers become, the more stalwart its editor needs to be. I know the harsh facts of today's newspaper economics have to be faced; that the greatest possible circulation is essential to viability. But if a newspaper is to be worth anything at all, so is the maintenance of its integrity and purpose.

Unfortunately 'the right to know' – a phrase coined in America – is not yet an accepted British concept. Its introduction is not agreeable to many people's present state of mind. They want *not* to know. There is at the best of times an aversion to disclosure, and an almost unqualified respect for privacy. These are not the best of times. Faced with international and national crises, some now beginning to impinge on his own personal affairs, already bewildered by a multiplicity of events demanding his attention, the average man's reaction to some new problem or scandal is all too often 'Why bring *that* up?'

If democracy is to be effective there is a great educational task to be done. These Lectures alert us to it. For in the end the final arbiter on all questions of freedom in a free country is not the Government, Parliament, the Law, the Church, or any other institutional authority. It is the climate of opinion. This climate is as variable as all others. But, being man-made, it can be altered. This is not a matter, moreover, in which the individual is completely powerless. We can all play a part in creating that climate. If to do so seems yet one more onerous responsibility, we can gird ourselves with Mr Justice Frankfurter's encouragement that 'The mark of a truly civilized man is confidence in the strength and security derived from the inquiring mind'.

In this matter of a nation's climate of opinion two recollections are apposite. The first shows that a nation can indicate what it is feeling about a particular subject, without having the least idea why it does so.

During the War the Director-General of the BBC found on his desk each week a figure indicating what the national audience had thought of the week's programmes as a whole two or three weeks earlier. One week the figure was so poor that I was sure there must have been a miscalculation. There had not been. I then asked whether any unusual programme had been broadcast that week. The answer was that the programmes had been very similar to those of the week before and the week after. (This was common in wartime.)

Reflecting on the aberration, I asked what had been the main news item of the week. The answer was the set-back at Arnhem.

This led me to ask for a graph to be drawn from the beginning of the war onwards, plotting the rise and fall of the public's appreciation of the BBC's programmes each week; the main news event of the week being listed underneath. The research people did this – and better. They were able also to graph a weekly morale index of the nation, which had been compiled on the same five-point scale: very good, good, indifferent, bad, very bad.

The result was startling. The two graphs were almost a pair of tram-lines. If the re-election of President Roosevelt sent up the spirits of the British nation by three points, then the nation had deemed the BBC's programmes for that week three points better. If a disaster caused gloom, the appreciation of the BBC's programmes dropped comparably. It was this experience which led me to say in my Haldane Lecture that 'The climate of a nation's opinion is more important than the opinions themselves'.

The other episode has in its aftermath persuaded me that a nation's character – on which its climate of opinion is largely based – is slow to change.

While General de Gaulle was in London during the War, he had, amidst all his preoccupations and difficulties, time – and the detachment – to reflect that if in 1940 the roles had been reversed, and it had been England that had fallen while France survived, the French broadcasting system would not have been able to do what the BBC had done. It could not have acted as host to all the exiled Governments and others wishing to broadcast from its shores to the peoples in their occupied countries, as well as developing a vast wartime world service of its own.

In his first period of office at the war's end he sent three officials to examine the possibility of setting up a French equivalent of the BBC. They questioned me about the professional independence of the BBC's news staff, about the liberty given to producers, about the powers of the Director-General, about the Director-General's relationship with the Governors, and that of the Governors with the Government. Was it true, I was asked, that the Prime Minister appointed all the Governors? I said it was. How then could it be said that the BBC was independent?

I explained that while, if the Prime Minister had to appoint a chairman of the BBC he might well appoint someone of his own party, the man would almost certainly be on the fringes of it. And over the whole of the Prime Minister's term of office it would as likely as not be found he had appointed slightly more Governors against his political persuasion than of it. I added that there were occasions when such conduct could seem Machiavellian, for my experience was that if any political issue came before the Board of Governors, the 'Conservative' Governors would bend over backwards to make sure justice was done to Labour, and the 'Labour' Governors would be equally zealous for fair treatment for the Conservatives.

The leader of the French delegation put his notes into his briefcase. 'Well, it's impossible,' he said.

'There are not seven Frenchmen like that.' And to this day French broadcasting is a tightly controlled Government system.

Even the most fervent supporter of Press freedom will be more effective if he occasionally adopts the stance of 'outside looking in'. There are both good and bad things to be seen. Lord Windlesham spoke of the ambivalence of the relationship between Government and the Media. One powerful ingredient of that relationship – particularly of the Broadcasting staffs, who are expected to be impartial – is the professionalism of the journalists and current affairs staffs. Their over-riding, indeed their sole, desire for effectiveness is something politicians find it hard to understand.

During Mr Attlee's first Government, when things began to go badly, three Cabinet Ministers visited me about what they said was the anti-Government bias in the BBC's Nine O'clock News. They suspected right-wing influence. I told them this was nonsense. The News staff's satisfaction could come only from a properly compiled and a well-written bulletin. This meant more to them than the fortunes of any Minister or Administration. I invited them to go and talk to the News staff. They came back, and withdrew their suspicions. It is very difficult for politicians to realize that not everyone is interested in politics.

This is a different issue from that of the broadcaster's widening their freedom to report politics. If, as Lord Windlesham believes, it was Suez that finally freed the politicians in Broadcasting, it was Granada's overturning of the barriers against dealing with the Rochdale by-election in 1958 that liberated the broadcasters. After that, nothing was the same again. Indeed there were times in the recent February General Election when one wondered if the pendulum had not swung too far Broadcasting's way.

I must confess I have long had doubts about the Lobbies as a means of keeping equilibrium between journalists and politicians. There is always the danger that the Parliamentary Lobby can be all too easy a way of covertly influencing the Press and Broadcasting. Also the Lobbies – and there are now far too many of them; they have spawned into other fields besides Politics – create divided loyalties. There is a loyalty to the giver of information, or non-information. There is a loyalty to the other Lobby journalists. There is a loyalty to the Lobby itself. A journalist's only loyalty should be to his editor.

These are lesser matters. Listening to the Lectures, and watching a pattern gradually emerging, one became conscious of a hidden strand, never mentioned, but brought even more to mind by the sincerity and integrity of the speakers. I will call it 'The Other side of Freedom'. Assuredly we must push the bounds of freedom for the Press and Broadcasting ever further, as Mrs Graham made clear. But journalists and broadcasters must realize that this freedom is not a personal privilege. Its purpose is to benefit the nation as a whole. It is a means to an end. That end is an informed and mature society. If that end is not served, and all too often it is not, then the Communicators will not deserve, or long command, the means. The opponents of freedom will never disappear. Freedom will be continually beset. It has to be continuously justified.

Nor can journalists ask their readers to take their claims to freedom of information seriously, if they are themselves prepared to dam its flow. Journalists and other staffs in newspaper offices who seek to act as censors, who deliberately disrupt production, who bring their newspapers near to ruin, cannot expect the public to regard their role as vital when they are seen to be subordinating it to the pursuit of their own interests. And while it may seem a counsel of perfection, the same is true of newspaper managements and unions who make publication subordinate to profits and leisure. Broadcasting has no silent days.

This introduction cannot close without some tribute to Granada. I opposed the introduction of commercial television with all the vigour I could command. I still think the Conservative Government's decision to establish it lost much of the broad educational potential of television in all spheres, including the arts. But there has been one mitigation of that defeat – Granada. Its political courage, its social investigations (World in Action and other programmes), its fearless exposure of issues, its alertness, and its imagination, may have drawn some official and unofficial rebukes. The rest of us can only cheer. Lord Bernstein, his colleagues, and the Granada staff have sought to uphold, so far as they have been permitted, 'Man's inalienable right to search for truth, no matter what orthodoxies he may challenge'. It has sometimes occurred to me that a good system of British broadcasting would have been two national public services, the one run by the BBC, the other by Granada.

One of the most imaginative of Granada's ventures is these Guildhall Lectures. For in an age when science and invention produce ever more advanced and complicated electronics, when an international conference is sitting in Geneva trying to agree on freedom of information transmitted by satellites, when Granada itself is a hive of computers and consoles, mixing panels and zoom lenses, feedbacks, playbacks, instant repeats, colour separation overlay, and I do not know what else, those controlling these marvels have realized that the simplest of all means of communication is still the best – people talking directly to people.

Words, unaccompanied by gadgetry, are still more powerful than anything else. They cannot be supplanted by pictures or typography, producers' or engineers' stunts, sounds or symbols. Words are mankind's only irreplaceable currency. All those in Broadcasting and Journalism, all of us without exception, have a trust to see they do not become devalued. Words are the armaments of freedom.

THE HALF FREE PRESS

THE HALF-FREE PRESS

by

HAROLD EVANS

WHEN I was invited to open this series of lectures, I was reminded of the report in the *New York World* which illustrates both the virtues of the freedom of the Press and my dilemma. The New York World reporter interviewed a celebrity at the airport and the following paragraph appeared in the newspaper:

> He was asked if he contemplated any further act of matrimony.
> 'Certainly', was his evasive reply.

I hope it is not thought to be evasion, but rather more fashionable confrontation, when I say that in talking about the freedom of the British Press I entitle this paper, 'The Half-Free Press'. I recognize at once that we have certain freedoms; after all, one can talk of freedom of the Press only in capitalist societies and even on a loose definition in only about one-fifth of the world. But I can best demonstrate the validity of my title with a true story.

Some of you may recognize the circumstances.

There is a scandal in the land. There is no sight of the substance of it, only the smell of something rotten. A newspaper makes inquiries. Painstakingly it builds up a dossier. It is about to publish a series of articles which give a glimpse of some of the truth when the law intervenes. The newspaper's facts, it is said, have some bearing on a series of legal cases which are technically before the courts. No trials have yet begun but until they have and until they are concluded, which in all their aspects may be several years, nothing can be published. To publish would be to trespass on the civil rights of the defendants and the jurisdiction of the law. It would be punishable as contempt of court; it would be a grievous abuse of the freedom of the press.

I am *not* referring to the thalidomide tragedy and the suppression on these grounds, of a major article prepared by *The Sunday Times*.

I am referring to Watergate: and I am describing what would have happened if Washington had been London. The first whiff of the scandal in the land was on the night of 17 June 1972, when five men with bugging equipment were caught in the offices of the Democratic national committee. From that moment, had Washington been London, the rules of contempt of court, the cry of *sub judice*, would have deterred independent press inquiry and prevented publication of any results. In Washington, however, the *Washington Post* was free, under American law, to play a major part in uncovering the scandal and it seized it brilliantly.

Two days after the original five burglars were arrested, the *Washington Post* confirmed a tenuous link between the burglars and the White House. On 1 August the *Post* reported a direct connection between the burglars, still awaiting trial, and Nixon campaign contributions.

For seven months, five of them months of the Presidential election the Watergate trial was *sub judice*. And that, in Britain, would have prevented the London *Times*, *Daily Express*, or whatever from publishing its attempts to unravel the links with the former Attorney-General, John Mitchell, because all this bore on the guilt of the Watergate burglars and all this was further complicated at different stages by new indictments.

But the *Washington Post* was free of legal inhibitions and it was only because it was free to go on printing revelations that the Democratic leadership was stirred to set up the Congressional inquiry. The full story – will we ever know the full story? – would never have begun to emerge without a combination, rather than a collision, between press and law, between press and the political process. What the free press did – free to make inquiries, free to publish – was to put Watergate on the nation's agenda and to create an atmosphere for truth. It is arguable, indeed, that had the rest of the American press and television followed that first lead of June 1972 as energetically as the *Washington Post*, so much more of the mess would have been revealed that in November 1972, Richard Nixon would have been defeated in the Presidential election.

Mrs Katharine Graham, who follows me in the Granada tumbril to this place of execution, will tell us in a few weeks about the ordeal and achievements of the *Washington Post* and others in the American Press. What I want to consider are the lessons for us.

It has been a comfort of ours, about the only one we have had recently, to say that this could not happen in Britain. Had Nixon been a British Prime Minister, he would have had to resign before the outrage of the House of Commons. But that piece of typically British smug self-congratulation assumes two things: first, that discussion or questions would have been allowed in Parliament. But Parliament in fact has its own *sub judice* rules. Second, and more fundamentally, it assumes that MPs would have known what the scandal was. And they would not. Parliament relies for much of its information on the press. When the press uncovers or dramatizes something, Parliament can sometimes prod very effectively: one thinks of the Commons Committee which followed *The Guardian*'s disclosures about the wages of blacks working for British firms in South Africa. Without *The Guardian* there would have been no Committee of MPs, reporting this week on the blacks in South Africa. This is not because MPs are complacent. It is simply that they do not have the resources to make continuous, detailed and expensive investigations. They look to the Press to do that. And, had the Watergate burglars been caught last week in Smith Square or Transport House, the half-free press of Britain would have been muzzled. Yet to talk of being muzzled is itself to make assumptions. Our Press might never have discovered what the real scandal was. Nye Bevan once said of the British Press that you cannot muzzle a sheep. In many areas that does us less than justice today, yet so used have we become to the constraints of contempt of court that we have long regarded any arrest as the moment to stop inquiries, not the moment to begin, and the existence of any legal proceedings as an assurance that truth will out. It is at least likely that for these reasons we would have got on the trail.

I am not saying that the London press would have suppressed Watergate. Had that complex and explosive series of revelations been left ticking as a parcel on any editor's desk, I dare say the most timid of us, the most respectful of due process, would have gladly risked a long term in Brixton to publish and be damned. That is too easy a proposition. What I am saying is that in Britain the press would have been chary of risking the penalties for contempt of court for the sake of an intriguing but apparently minor story, for that is all the *Washington Post* pursued, at first, in June 1972 and that is all with hindsight.

We might all reflect: what would have happened in London if, after all, a brave or ignorant editor had published something like that June 1972 report in a British context? The editor would not have been able to plead that the crime of Watergate reached to the highest in the land. He would not have known. What would have happened after the inevitable prosecution by the Attorney-General, the heavy fine or imprisonment, the reply by the Lord Chief Justice and the scandalized letters to the *Times*? Would other editors have rushed in where one seemed to have blundered? Would the IBA have allowed World in Action to do the same thing? Would the BBC Governors have unleashed Man Alive?

In a word, No. There is a real difficulty here, for let us remember that what we are talking about in the *Washington Post* reporting is, in the British context, contempt of court in a *criminal* case. The *Washington Post* was, possibly, prejudicing the jury against innocent men by pronouncing on their associations.

I will discuss later how the British Press might be enabled to deal with a Watergate. But, for the moment, contrast what happened after Watergate with thalidomide. In thalidomide we at the *Sunday Times* have been challenging contempt of court in a civil case where no jury trial is likely, where no one's liberty is at stake. It goes without saying that in America if publication pending a criminal trial by jury is possible, with public benefit, it would be unthinkable there for information to be suppressed because of a civil trial before a judge. It ought to be unthinkable here that we cannot analyse or discuss or argue the facts about something that happened nearly thirteen years ago for the simple reason that the courts are said to be seized of the matter. Some seizure.

At the *Sunday Times* we are no longer concerned to persuade the drug's makers, Distillers, who have, in the end, done the decent thing on compensation for the children. We are concerned to get at the truth about how the tragedy occurred – no, two tragedies, the medical tragedy and the legal tragedy. For the lawyers still meet but individual parents and their children still do not know how much money they will receive. But the 400-plus children who were born deformed are entering their teens and they and the public are no nearer to knowing why they were affected. This is the biggest drug disaster of our modern times. In Britain mothers took the drug on the advice of their National Health doctors. But I cannot tonight even hazard a guess when you the public will be able to consider how we think it all happened. The ruling of the House of Lords which banned our report on the origins of the tragedy, which we wanted to publish in 1972 means that while there is a single writ there cannot be a single revelation. And one action is, I understand, still being continued which may mean several years.

Perhaps the Phillimore Committee examining our contempt laws will recommend abolishing civil contempt; perhaps then Parliament will legislate on Phillimore. Perhaps then we shall be freed of the Order imposed by the Lords Spiritual and Temporal in the Court of Parliament of Her Majesty The Queen assembled. But whatever happens about contempt, I can tell you tonight that our banned article has to escape further snares. The article quotes from internal memoranda of Distillers Biochemicals Ltd., the subsidiary which made the drug. Distillers, who have always denied negligence, know that we are quoting from their own internal documents because we asked them to comment. They responded, as they always have in this story, by reaching for their lawyers. They say they will take legal action to stop us from quoting their documents because the words in the documents are their copyright. Secondly, they will try to stop us even indirect reporting of the contents, which they say would be a breach of confidence.

Most of us would recognize there are good grounds for the law of confidence – those between a master and servant during employment, between a solicitor and his client, a doctor and his patient, etc.

The law, however, also suggests that there may be cases where public interest can over-ride private confidence. We argued as much in court where an attempt was made to stop us publishing a confidential document from a public relations firm which claimed to have a British MP working for them behind the scenes on behalf of the Greek military government.

These two legal challenges of copyright and confidence appeared, but we did not announce them, during our contempt actions with the Attorney-General. They were not then, for obvious reasons, our main concern.

We therefore undertook to give Distillers at least three days' notice if we intended to use their documents and meanwhile we would not publish. Since the House of Lords went 5–0 against us we have been preparing our arguments on the law of copyright and the law of confidence, and drawing up a list of all the documents we have. It has been a long job because there are very many complex documents about this drug and how it was made, but I can tell you that we have now completed that exercise. I have therefore celebrated the occasion of these lectures by writing today to Distillers' lawyers to end the moratorium. When those actions are heard they will be of great importance for the freedom of the Press to investigate matters of public concern.

Now all these things we are attempting to do which should have been done in 1961, but there has never been a public inquiry. One thinks immediately of Aberfan; now of the Isle of Man Summerland fire disaster. Though with Summerland there is a civil action in which negligence is alleged, there is also a public inquiry.

All these years in thalidomide there have been judgements on policy to which the undisclosed truth of the thalidomide case is vital. There have been judgements on safety standards in drugs, on attitudes to civil liability on advertising, on relations between family doctors and drug companies. A Private Member's Bill before the Commons in 1972 proposed a new definition of the legal liabilities of drug companies. It was defeated. Now we have a Royal Commission under Lord Pearson on Civil Liability. It cannot be right that decisions are made in these and other instances in ignorance of the *Sunday Times* researches.

Leaving it to the courts was always a rotten idea because most writs never end in trial and because even when they do this is a long and costly way of getting at the truth. The civil law encourages settlements, not a relentless search for truth. In the vast majority of instances that serves society. But there are cases like thalidomide, and like Summerland, where it does not serve society. This is where we come to one of the more curious aspects of the law of the land on contempt of court, as it must now be understood following the House of Lords judgement against us. Three of the five Law Lords said that the Press can argue a moral case as we did at the beginning of our campaign on thalidomide even when litigation is pending. Lord Devlin, a former Chairman of the Press Council and Lord of Appeal, has said that this is a marked advance on what existed before. In some respects it may be. But if argument is permitted, production of the evidence on which it is based is not. Once a writ is issued there must be no reporting of fact, according to the Law Lords, because it might prejudge the issues. The Law Lords would not concede that after serving a writ there could be any question of striking a balance between the requirements of the courts in preserving the legal

[29]

cocoon and the public benefit in disclosure and discussion.

There were some vague and utterly impractical remarks about not wishing the Press to be gagged by the mere issue of a writ. But that ruling of the Law Lords could, on unhelpful interpretations, lead to a suppression of reporting in Britain on matters of the greatest public importance. If tomorrow, for instance, the *Times* reported an allegation of massacre in Mozambique, the issue of a writ for libel could now be held, in English law, to prevent *The Times* and other newspapers from justifying their attitude with further evidence. It would be all right to argue; it is illegal to adduce the evidence on which the argument is based.

I hope I have demonstrated the wide gap in but two legal areas between the freedom of the press of the United States and the half-free press of Britain and before I comment on further areas where the British press is restricted by comparison with several other countries, not only the United States, before I suggest the forms of contempt.

I should acknowledge that on occasion the British press has shown a frantic ingenuity which has produced some splendid examples of what I can only call nudge and wink journalism.

I quote:

Stout balding Mr John Jones, cashier to a firm of textile converters was missing yesterday from his home in Cemetery Avenue, Openshaw.
Round the corner in Funeral Street, Mr Henry Brown said he had not seen his blonde attractive wife Mamie since the week-end.

A director of the firm which employs Mr Jones said yesterday that the firm's books would have been due for audit next week. Mr Jones was also treasurer of the local Working Men's Holiday Fund.

Neighbours described Mrs Brown as a gay girl. It is understood that she and Mr Jones were close friends.

At a flat in Southpool, stout balding Mr Arthur Smith said he had never heard of Mr Jones of Openshaw. Blonde attractive Mrs Dolly Smith said she had never been known as Mamie Brown. Early yesterday police were seeking to interview a stout, bald-headed man whom they believed could be of assistance to them in their inquiries into a case of fraudulent conversion.

A man accompanied police to Southpool police station. Blows were exchanged in Southpool's High Street after a man ran at high speed along the street. Police ran at high speed along the street after a man.

Later a man was detained. A man will appear in court today.

The headline to this, alas fictional example*, must be:

LATER A MAN WAS DETAINED.

But back to the hard benches of the court house.

First, contempt of court in criminal cases. How can we allow for the exceptional instances where the present rules of contempt lead to suppression with ill consequences without at the same time risking the

* By John Townsend of *The Guardian*

very precious right to a fair trial? I suggest that we can get out of the strait jacket by permitting a general defence that publication may be necessary in public interest. There is some authority for this in Australian judgements and it has been hinted at in some leading English cases. It does not take me all the way but I would go along on the judgement of Justice Owen in a New South Wales case: 'If in the course of the ventilation of a question of public concern matter is published which may prejudice a party in the conduct of a lawsuit, it does not follow that a contempt has been committed.' And then a little later: 'The discussion of public affairs . . . cannot be required to be suspended merely because the discussion . . . may, as an incidental but not intended by-product, cause some likelihood of prejudice to a person who happens at the time to be a litigant.'

The newspaper which took the risk of pleading this new defence of public interest would have to demonstrate that it reasonably believed the public benefit would be so promoted by publication as to offset any prejudice to a fair trial which might result. The burden would be on the newspaper to justify its departure from the normal rules, and that defence would succeed only in exceptional cases.

I must say that I was shocked when I worked in San Francisco and followed a 'trial by newspaper'. A man called Rexinger was arrested and long before his trial date was headlined in the San Francisco newspapers as 'The Murderer'. And since it was a sexual case his guilt was blazingly transparent when a newspaper was able to reveal that Rexinger had, at some stage, written poetry:

Fortunately for him, he was not only a poet, but discovered to be innocent before the trial when somebody else confessed, and he was released 'without a stain on his character' as they say.

My proposed change in the law would not help the San Francisco papers if they were published here, nor would it in any way have saved either the *Daily Mirror* or *The Sunday Times* in two leading cases for contempt of court. The new defence would not have saved Silvester Bolam from going to prison in 1949 for his sensational *Mirror* splash in which he described John George Haigh, accused of acid bath murders, as a Vampire and, obviously guilty. Nor would public interest defence have saved *The Sunday Times* £5,000 for accidentally revealing in an article on race relations that Michael X had been a brothel keeper, procurer, and property racketeer. Michael X was awaiting a retrial, the implications of which we overlooked. No newspaper that I know wants the freedom for pre-trial reporting in cases like that, still less to do a Vampire splash, and they would not have it, under my proposal.

The defence of public interest could rarely be used but it would have got a reasonable certainty of public benefit. This is not rhetoric, for there are clever people who have learned to exploit the law of contempt. I have on my desk at the moment an Insight memo on a series of national consumer frauds operated through network-linked companies. It has none of the drama of Watergate, but there is a real public interest.

People are being robbed of their money. They are being brought up for trial around the country. They plead guilty. This suits the manipulators because there is a small fine, an easily bearable expense, and the ramifications of their operations are not revealed. The fraud cannot be revealed in a newspaper because still more individuals associated with this linked group of companies are awaiting criminal trial and the prejudice arising from these related events, it is said, would unjustly be visited on them if we publish. Moreover, each little local trial produces a number of new actions, so widespread is the call for a period of *sub judice*. At least, one action has been outstanding at every point since September 1969, and even if no new cases are brought from now it will be 1975/6 before the current charges are cleared up.

We at the *Sunday Times* have not yet decided our own attitude to this story – is there a tipstaff in the house? But my modest reform would make the risks of publication more nearly tolerable.

There is a second improvement we must make to the law of contempt. We must give a decent funeral to the doctrine of imminence. Most people accept that once there is a criminal charge we should all shut up, subject to considering the exceptional new defence of public interest. But how many people realize that at the moment the law goes further than this? It says that we should also shut up when we know or suspect a charge or an arrest is 'imminent'. Here is an instance.

In July 1966 the *Sunday Times* and the *Daily Mail* documented a car insurance swindle operated by a Dr Emil Savundra, remember, which had affected thousands of motorists. Dr Savundra had left the country. We named another director also, called Stuart Walker; he left the country shortly after we published without hindrance. There was no talk of proceedings against either man. On 14 January 1967, Savundra returned to Britain. He was not, to our surprise, arrested. He moved freely. He re-occupied his expensive home. More than two weeks later, bold as brass, he appeared on television on the Frost Programme to answer the allegations the *Sunday Times* and *Daily Mail* had made against him. He had a rough time on the programme – I did not care for it myself – but he was able to make statements without challenge which we knew to be wrong. Our inquiries about whether Savundra was to be prosecuted fell on stony ground. On Sunday, 6 February, therefore, we published some of the things Dr Savundra had said, and we commented on them point by point. Seven days after the programme and five days after our article, Savundra was charged. But that was nearly a month since his return to Britain, and many months after we had given a full report in the newspapers.

He and Walker later appealed against their subsequent convictions on the grounds that the air had been poisoned against them by publicity before the trial. The appeals were dismissed, but the then Lord Justice Salmon attacked us for our report and he issued a severe warning that the doctrine of imminence still had teeth.

Imminence is an increasing problem because of the opportunities today for business and consumer rackets, because of the speed at which the operators work and their capacity for leaving a trail of false footprints for the overworked Fraud Squad.

There are not infrequently cases where the evidence may not justify a criminal charge, but where the practice is so sharp that the public needs to be warned very loudly and quickly. Only the press can do that. How long should the newspaper wait while the sharp practice continues? How long is imminence? How long is a piece of string? In the draft of this talk I next gave a current example but our lawyers wrote in. 'Delete. This case will probably still be *sub judice* when you speak and the context of "scandal investigation" could be prejudicial.' I am taking that advice on this occasion – you here tonight would not want to be witness to a felony.

Of course the Press can remain active and chance its arm over imminence. But it is a gratuitous risk. There should be more certainty in the law. The law of contempt should operate only from the moment of charge, which is often, of course, some considerable time before a trial. And do not forget that the individual who is named is protected rightly by the law of libel.

I now turn to contempt in civil cases where reform is less difficult. We should, first, adopt the public interest defence that I have suggested for criminal cases. But that is not enough. Contempt here, whether before a judge or before a jury, should surely run only from the moment of trial, or the setting down of a date for trial, and it should not begin years before with the issue of a writ, as it has in thalidomide. That view of the balance between the requirements of justice and reasonable public

[36]

discussion is too mechanistic. I agree that witnesses, litigants, and courts, should be protected against intimidation, misrepresentation of evidence or publication of prejudgements on the legal issues of the trial. But there should be no hindrance to the free flow of information. That would, of course, enable us to publish our thalidomide article, but nothing very frightening would happen in general practice. We already have the system in one area of our life which provokes sustained and vehement comment and uninhibited reporting in what is a quasi-judicial context. I refer to planning inquiries. No one suggests that the inspector (alias the judge) or the parties or witnesses need to be protected by archaic rules relating to contempt of court. Moreover not one of the cases quoted against us, and they went back to 1740, were concerned with a straightforward newspaper investigation on a matter of public importance.

We have now at last reached the central dilemma of the British attitude to press freedom and some of the assumptions that have run half-clothed through this lecture. Our philosophy and, in turn our law and our attitudes have been conditioned to defend free speech rather than free inquiry. I have shown how in the House of Lords judgement it has been ruled that it is all right to utter opinion but not to publish the evidence that one believes sustains the opinion. We have a press which is half free, I believe, because its needs and the needs of the society it serves have outgrown a philosophy rooted in the simpler virtues of free expression. Reality today requires ethical justification for free inquiry and for unimpeded publication of fact rather than of opinion. The Americans already have a phrase: The Right to Know. It is almost un-English, for we rely on the liberal defence of free expression so memorably bequeathed to us by Milton, Locke and Mill.

Truth is good for men, and truth will emerge if all discussion is submitted to the powerful test of the reason of the rational man. Free expression is a natural right for human dignity and happiness. You know that. I agree with it too but it is not enough. The ethic is too much centred on the rights of free speech, too much concerned with the individual's opinions. This is understandable, historically. Much of last century's newspaper was a pamphlet of opinions rather than a journal of news. It was invective, not investigation, that got the early newspapers into trouble and needed to be justified. George III clapped John Wilkes in The Tower for his diatribe not for his documents. Even some of the greatest utterances by newspapermen, have been powered by a defence of free opinion. 'The first duty of the Press is to obtain the earliest and most correct intelligence of the events of the time, and instantly, by disclosing them to make them the common property of the nation.' Every copy-boy knows of the famous words of *The Times* of 6 February 1852, attributed to Delane, but written in fact by Robert Lowe and Henry Reeve. Often editors get the credit for things they do not really write, and sometimes the blame...

But it was not, as might appear from a paraphrase, called for in defence of some right of investigation and disclosure. What had happened was that Lord Derby had attacked *The Times* for its *opinions* on

Louis Napoleon. 'It is incumbent on the Press', he said, 'to maintain that tone of moderation and respect even in expressing frankly their opinions on foreign affairs which would be required of every man who pretends to guide public opinion.' Statesmen, it said, deal mainly with rights and interests; the Press with opinions and sentiments.

It was just seven years after *The Times* leader that John Stuart Mill said that the Government or a popular majority should not be permitted 'to prescribe opinions' to the public or to determine 'what doctrines or what arguments they shall be allowed to hear.'

The peculiar evil which robbed the human race, was 'silencing the expression of an opinion'. It was on this basis that an independent press erected its defences for the next 100 years. Every word of what Mill said stands today but the modern press cannot survive or achieve full freedom simply by arguing from the classical virtues of free speech. There will not be a murmur of dissent about John Stuart Mill from men and women who daily, in government, law and all centres of power restrict the flow of information or stamp 'confidential' on the documents. They believe in freedom of speech as passionately as any journalist. What they have not perceived or been convinced of is that only with the freest flow of facts is freedom of opinion of much value. The assumption of Mill and the Liberals was that there was a free flow of intelligence just as the classical economists assumed a perfect market and free competition. Nobody wrote about guaranteeing the free flow of information. It was, for one thing, an infinitely smaller problem.

Government and security were less complex. In the newspapers the élite simply argued with the élite.

Today the press must be sustained by what it does for society, this very different society, rather than by simply what it does for the soul of the individual. It certainly remains for the Press a virtue to ventilate opinion. Concentration of control imposes on us today duties of greater access for the public so that we escape the jibe of Huey Long about Henry Luce: 'The owner of *Time* Magazine', said Long, 'is like the owner of a shoe shop who stocks only the shoes to fit *hisself*'. But it is not by diversity of opinion that the press can defend its claims. It is by its interpretation and description of reality, and it is in this area that we in Britain are so bedevilled. We all of us live in what Walter Lippmann called 'an invisible environment' – a world where without a great continuing flow of information we are blind and defenceless. We can see and understand our visible world of home and neighbourhood; but we cannot without a free Press know of the planning decision which will bring a motorway through the back garden; or the circumstances why our children are not learning to read properly; or why a quarrel in the middle-east should stop our machinery and darken our homes. Governments as well as citizens need a free and inquiring Press. With a volatile, pluralistic electorate, and a complex bureaucracy, a free press provides an indispensable feedback system from governed to the governing, from consumers to producers, from the regions to the centre, and not least from one section of the bureaucracy to another.

The heads of the police themselves did not know, before *The Times* revealed it, of the corruption among certain elements of the police. Many company chairmen did not know, until they read it in *The Guardian*, about the conditions in their own South African subsidiaries. The Governors of the BBC must have read with astonishment the *News of the World* allegations about graft and sexual corruption to promote the playing of records.

Governments cannot govern well without reliable reporting and criticism. They do not have the knowledge. No intelligence system, no bureaucracy, can offer the information provided by competitive reporting; the cleverest secret agents of the police state are inferior to the plodding reporter of the democracy. It is one of the strengths of society with a competent and plural system of free communication that feedback happens automatically. Every political lawyer and bureaucrat understands this about trade, that the feedback of customers exercising choice is a corrective mechanism for the manufacturer. Every politician and bureaucrat professes to believe it about government, but in office persuades himself that the limitations of information he imposes or accepts are imperceptible or necessary for national security relations with foreign governments, the preservation of the latest coalitions.

As William Haley once said, everybody believes in freedom of information until it runs into his own vested interest, whether he be a Minister or a trade union leader, or a bishop or the secretary of a professional body. But concealment corrodes the chance of creating confidence between governed and governing, manager and managed. It induces alienation. People come to identify the state or local government not with themselves, but with something remote and incomprehensible. Secrecy creates anxieties and suspicions that outweigh any temporary convenience. Consider for a moment the consequences in the coal dispute of the one that is still going on, the last Government's early refusal to reveal the figures of coal stocks at power stations. What a holiday that provided for conspiracymongers; what a diversion from the real debate. The facts, when the *Sunday Times* secured them – independently – did not suggest at all that the government had perpetrated a massive confidence trick, but in the atmosphere of needless secrecy we, too, were assailed because the facts did not fit the conspiracy theories.

Still moving via those coalstocks from the general to the particular, I must make it clear that when I talk of Government I am talking of successive British Governments. Successive in the last ten years, not of Governments which might succeed in the next ten months. The last Government set up commissions on contempt, libel and secrecy which were a hopeful initiative; so has been the marginal increase of Green Papers. But we are dabbling and the problem is wider than a simple and inevitable tension between any government and any press. Lord Windlesham, who speaks next in this series of lectures, has said in his scholarly book *Communication and Political Power**, that the restrictions the communicator must accept are 'only an outer boundary fence inside which he must keep'. I beg to differ. They permeate our

* Johnathan Cape, London 1966

[42]

daily life; they are the hardened arteries of our society. The suffocation that results from habits of secrecy and suppression is not generally realized by people who do not have to deal with them every day of their lives. I believe it underlies some of the divisions and some of the muddle we experience. The Press, of course, is the object of some popular suspicion.

There are certainly exaggerated ideas about our powers. Newspapers have no more rights than the ordinary citizen. We are not detectives with rights of search. We are not civil servants with powers under regulations to know about anybody's property, income or family. We are not Parliamentarians with rights to summon witnesses and to protection for our privileges. We do not seek all these rights. But we would certainly like to be relieved of some of the restraints based on the exercise of an ordinary citizen's rights to know. We must keep within the law of libel, the law of trespass, of slander, of confidence, of copyright, of contempt of court, of Parliamentary privilege (and I have been up before a privilege committee) and the bureaucrats all-purpose chastity belt, the Official Secrets Act. Anyone who suspects exaggeration in my description of attitudes in public life should consider how often even that much-praised institution of Parliamentary question time fails to elicit answers or even gets a blank refusal. Or, better still, read the evidence from the civil servants in the unhappy Franks report on Official Secrets when Sir Burke Trend (now Lord Trend), the Secretary to the Cabinet, explains why he and others are against what he calls 'the business of striptease of a Government'.

One of the ironies of the Franks Report was that when these civil servants' evidence came to be published there was serious representation in Whitehall that revealing the evidence would itself be a breach of the Official Secrets Act which has not yet been reformed. It is not seven veils they want; it is seventy-seven (complete with padlocks). Of course all of us in the Press recognize that the business of government could not be carried on if every internal memo were released and that there are areas of national security which require secrecy. Our demands are modest but misrepresented. We are tired of being fobbed off with the *bon mot* of US Justice Holmes that we cannot claim the right to shout fire in a crowded lecture theatre. We do not claim it. We do not press for openness in negotiation but we repudiate concealment in policy making. We recognize there are large differences of judgement. If we had the access to public files of Swedes or Americans we would be happy to have provision for the executive to appeal to the courts for restriction, as the US Information Act of 1966 allows. But good intentions are not enough. They evaporate under heat.

For the rest, I will be brief. Minor charges could be made but I do not protest tonight about the law of libel. Those who do strenuously protest are usually the casual purveyors of character assassination. I certainly regard American law following the case of the *New York Times* versus Sullivan as unfair to men in public life. The law of slander is more troublesome for investigative journalism because reporters have to ask pointed questions. Threats of slander suits were used against the *Sunday Times* when we began asking questions about the Southern Counties Car Insurance Company.

They were used with even greater vigour when we began to look at the profits of Robert Maxwell's Pergamon Press. Normally the defence is to prove the truth of the defamatory question but at the stage of asking questions one may not have the admissible evidence. No doubt damages in these circumstances would be small, but such cases are often not meant to come to court. They are meant to waste time and confuse the issue.

It is, in the end, the cumulative effect of all these laws which is so frustrating and so conducive to encouraging an unhealthy furtiveness in British life. It is absurd that I should have been cautioned by Scotland Yard under the Official Secrets Act for publishing an official paper canvassing abolition of half of the railway system. It is even more saddening that a rank and file delegate at the Tory Conference deplored our publication because he said it was *before* the policy had been decided. Precisely.

Finally, there are public records and the tendency of too many local authorities of all kinds to do what they can in private. It is no exaggeration to say our records, and the habits of some of the local authorities, are often allowed to protect inefficiency, injustice and sometimes corruption. The records at Companies House are laxly filed and years out of date. People in this country are still allowed to hide behind nominee shareholdings. It is extremely difficult for the Press to expose property rackets, because we need the permission of the owner to inspect the records of the Land Registry. And we have no official way of checking who pays the rates.

It is added reason for dismay about Watergate that the disclosures about the San Clemente White House, about the funding of Creep, and about Robert Vesco's campaign money, were possible only by diligent use of public federal and state records of the kind that are not available in Britain.

If I am right about the proper role of the Press today, there is a failing on two sides, for it has to be acknowledged that there is a shortcoming in our press performance in the way we live up to the doctrine of social responsibility I sketched earlier. It was during years of neglect by all the mainland British Press that the seeds of violence were sown in Ulster. Part of our weakness has been due to the philosophy of free speech we picked up, part to our slow emergence from, in Walter Lippmann's phrase, a minor craft to an under-developed profession. But we have, I think, made strides and are too often blamed for the excesses of a different time. We need now to develop the intellectual and moral disciplines of a profession. If we dig more diligently we must not devalue so-called routine reporting. We cannot claim greater access if we ignore what is available or diminish its worth because it is not half-concealed. We must not allow our necessary scepticism to degenerate into cynicism. We cannot claim our rights simply as entertainers, though boring we do not want to be. We cannot claim them if we intrude too many of our own views. We must always correct error; but at the same time we must resist the ideas that only the perfect Press is entitled to be free. The right to be free means the right to be free.

A wary man can discern a number of smudges on the horizon for the Press. By no means all of our difficulties are due to Government or law or restriction. But if we in the half-free Press are to fulfil the role society needs, and half expects, we must at least be enabled to do the best we can.

GOVERNMENT AND THE MEDIA

GOVERNMENT AND THE MEDIA:
FALLACIES OF CONFUSION

by

LORD WINDLESHAM

IN the present situation may I recommend to you, Sir William, and to others who share your interest in literature and political behaviour, Jeremy Bentham's *Handbook of Political Fallacies*? Here they all are, carefully spelt out and classified, the techniques of obstruction and delay, together with the respectable sounding reasons which are customarily advanced in their support. There are old favourites like the procrastinators argument; or 'Wait a Little, This is not the Time' and the snail's pace argument or 'One Thing at a Time! Not too fast'. Laudatory personalities are contrasted with vituperative personalities and both are linked with issues: 'the persons who propose or promote the measure are bad, therefore the measure is bad and ought to be rejected'. Custom and distrust and prejudice are also examined. It is all very timely and with the recent Election fresh in our minds we might be tempted to add one or two home truths about public opinion polls and the contribution made by bookmakers to the political scene. But in turning over in my mind the subject of this year's series of Guildhall lectures it was only when I got to Part The Fourth of the Handbook that I knew I had reached home. It is headed 'Fallacies of Confusion'. When all else fails, and discussion of an issue can no longer be avoided, there is always the last standby: consciously or otherwise the resort to misleading or fallacious arguments the result of which is to perplex and obscure.

Confusion, or misunderstanding, or what is currently described as non-communication is undoubtedly a characteristic of relations between Government and the media. Sometimes it will arise from straightforward conflicts of interest; Governments often want to keep quiet many of the things which the media want to disclose. Sometimes the suspicion or resentment that is latent at both ends of the relationship erupts into open hostility. From time to time there are efforts both by the politicians and by the media to mitigate this. It is particularly apt that one of the most notable of these was Granada's recent series of programmes on *The State of the Nation*, a television inquiry into the working of Parliament.

But despite ventures of this kind misunderstandings persist. Even if the existence of confusion is not too hard to identify in the relations between Government and the media the fallacies which underly so much of the confusion are elusive and difficult to pin down. One of the main causes, as it seems to me, can be found in the constant reiteration of vague generalities and catch-phrases which are seldom pursued closely. Harold Evans was right to point out in his first lecture in this series that the theme of the freedom of the Press itself provides an example. Much lip service is paid to the ideal of a free Press, but noble sentiments of this kind have a habit of receding into the background when a particular interest, political or otherwise, becomes involved. We need not, I think, be too censorious about this since in practice the Press in this country is maintained in a state of relative freedom (if I can avoid distinguishing the notches which mark the yardstick between 'free' and 'half-free') not by adherence to any ideological standard, but by a shifting balance between conflicting interests. Freedom of the Press is a state of affairs as well as a state of mind.

At the time of an Election the pattern changes. The Press and broadcast media are dealing not with Government but with Party. Most of the leading figures are the same but the relationship is altered in many ways. The Government Information Services withdraw almost completely from the stage. Few ministerial decisions are taken and the flow of official announcements dwindles to a trickle. It is a long standing convention, accepted by both major Parties, that during a General Election campaign nothing is done by the Government Information machine to detract attention from the Parties. When the Prime Minister meets the Press each day during the campaign he does so at his own Party headquarters. The Press Office at No 10 grows silent. Nor will any other Minister put out statements on matters of potential controversy through his own Departmental Press Office. When, for instance, the January trade figures were published jointly by the Central Statistical Office and the Department of Trade and Industry on 25 February the comments of the then Chancellor of the Exchequer were handled entirely through Party channels.

In the course of an Election campaign the volume of public comment by Ministers in their capacity as Party politicians expands greatly. Contact with the Press becomes closer and more intimate. As has recently been demonstrated the desire of the politician to make his voice heard in the weeks before a General Election is more than matched by the readiness of the media to provide opportunities for him to do so. No longer is it necessary, as it was for Reith in the early days of the BBC, for broadcasting to struggle for what he called 'recognition and opportunity' in the political arena. Half a century later the determination of the broadcaster not to be left standing on the side-line but to play an active part in the democratic process is a phenomenon that emerges most clearly at Election time. In the television coverage of the February 1974 Election (I was going to say the 1974 Election, but in case there is another one, I'd better say the February 1974 Election) we have seen this determination take the form of the most extensive output that has ever been devoted to any British General Election. Whether or not the volume of the coverage amounted to a case of over-kill is a question that will be debated for a long time. My own impression is that it seemed in some ways greater than it was because of the wide variety of programmes and the fact that most of them were transmitted in the main evening viewing times.

Already agreed were the daily Election broadcasts under the direct control of the Parties; fourteen in England, and one each in Scotland and Wales. Then there were the special Election programmes produced by the BBC, ITN and the Independent Television programme companies, regional as well as network, as a systematic and planned coverage of a major event of national importance. These included, as their climax, the highly professional coverage of the Election results on 28 February and 1 March. But in addition, the regular scheduled current affairs programmes remained on the air. As one edition followed another it soon became evident that *Panorama*, *This Week*, *Nationwide*, *Today*, *World in Action*, *Midweek*, *Weekend World* and *The Money Programme* were adopting the Election, if not as their sole subject at least as a major topic of continuing interest. It is quite understandable that they should do so; indeed most politicians would feel that it showed commendable good judgement. The consequence was that between 7 and 27 February – a period of twenty days – (excluding the Party Election broadcasts) 30 hours and 25 minutes were devoted to Election coverage on Independent Television. During the same period, in the case of BBC Television, politicians appeared on the screen for a total of 11 hours 36 minutes (that is just the time occupied by politicians themselves appearing on the screen). This figure, which again excludes Party Election broadcasts, is based on a special count conducted by the BBC and is restricted to the personal appearances of politicians on television, for example, making speeches, answering questions at Press conferences or being interviewed. The BBC radio networks were also hard at work. In addition to the coverage on news bulletins and current affairs programmes, there was a new development. Each morning for thirteen days, 55 minutes were devoted to Election Call on Radio 4 – a total of 11 hours 55 minutes with large numbers of individual calls each morning. This was the first time in an Election campaign that there had been direct contact via the broadcast media, between Party Leaders and electors on anything approaching this scale.

No one can yet say what influence television had on the outcome. But this is too good an opportunity to miss to put forward one or two early observations. I offer these thoughts to those who are now engaged in post-mortems in Party Headquarters, irrespective of which side of Smith Square they may be situated, and broadcasting organizations. Nor should we overlook the ever-optimistic academics who have taken on the awesome task of trying to interpret electoral behaviour in terms of political science. I suggest that it would be a mistake to be diverted by the debate over the extent of the coverage from the truth that it is what is said and by whom that really matters. But can over-exposure encourage cynicism on the part of the audience of viewer-voters? Do experienced television reporters and producers influence the choice of issues and the way in which they are perceived? Most important of all, has the tone in which so much political debate has been conducted on television, and not just at an Election, brought credit or discredit to the practice of politics? Is it necessary that the conventions of political broadcasting should result in transposing to the media the confrontation style of politics which marks the proceedings on the floor of the House of Commons? Does the present system encourage a strictly limited form of argument along the lines of 'Yes, I did', 'No, you didn't', which can do as much to obscure as to reveal the truth of what a politician is trying to say?

Having itemized some questions for others to answer it is time I got on with my own central theme for this evening's lecture. It can be briefly stated. The starting point is an assessment of what Governments can expect of the media and what the media can expect of Governments. The question I have asked myself is why is it that so many people working in the media feel that the Government is bearing down on them unduly influencing their reporting and comment on the news, while at the same time many equally honourable men in Government believe that the Press and the broadcast media lie in wait, ready to trip them up, to distort what they say, and generally to make their task of communicating with the public more difficult? I should warn you at this point that the answer to this question, if there is one, will not follow for another twenty or thirty minutes.

Let us go back to the beginning. Democracy depends on discussion and debate. Decisions which are not democratically arrived at will not in the long term, or even in the short term, endure. Government, on the other hand, depends on consent. To obtain consent for their policies Ministers and their political supporters must endeavour to make their voices heard. Thus they need the media. They must explain. They must seek to persuade. They are entitled, as part of the process of democratic Government, to make the most of the opportunities open to them, and to search out new opportunities to communicate with the public. Some of these channels are institutionalized. The Parliamentary Lobby is an example. Press and politicians, each confined within the precincts of the Palace of Westminster have built up over many years a working relationship which is of advantage to both. Conventions develop and are mutually accepted.

The Lobby currently contains about 125 political correspondents who have access to the Members' Lobby outside the Chamber of the House of Commons. This group is distinct from the reporters in the Parliamentary Press Gallery whose task is to put on record the actual debates in both Houses of Parliament. Contact between the Government and the Lobby is close and frequent and almost always on a non-attributable basis. In the last Parliament Lobby briefings generally took place twice a day when the House was sitting. These were normally conducted by the Prime Minister's Chief Press Secretary or by one of his assistants, either in Downing Street or in the Houses of Parliament. Each Thursday after making a statement on forthcoming business in the House of Commons, the Leader of the House met the Lobby. I doubt if the present arrangements are very different. These regular encounters are, of course, only one feature of the network of contacts which a Lobby correspondent will build up with Ministers, as well as with backbenchers and with Government spokesmen. Although it has not been above criticism, particularly from those who observe politics from Fleet Street rather than from Westminster, the Lobby system continues to function as a main channel of political communication. Day in and day out it is the source of substantial volume of reporting and comment on the national news and national politics in general. It is, moreover, a channel which is familiar to all Ministers and Parliament and one that is equally accessible to Government and Opposition.

Other specialist groups of journalists with whom the Government have regular contact, such as foreign and diplomatic correspondents, industrial correspondents, city editors and economic correspondents, also have regular briefing meetings with the Departments and the Ministers mainly concerned.

Any Minister who is charged with special responsibility for Government Information will find himself to be the recipient of complaints by his Ministerial colleagues and by his Party's supporters in Parliament and outside Parliament for that matter, about the way in which the Government's case is presented in the media. It will not surprise you to learn that such complaints are frequent and that they are often accompanied by requests to intervene with the managements concerned. My own response to these requests when I had this responsibility differed with the circumstances, but as a guiding principle I in no way regarded myself as bound to forward complaints, whatever their origin, unless I had some reason for believing, after making inquiries, that they might have some substance. Sometimes a complaint seemed to me to be justified. On other occasions it originated from lack of knowledge of the media, or upon selective information, or most common of all upon an apprehension of something that might be said and by whom, rather than what had been said. The most significant characteristic of these representations was that nine out of ten of the complaints referred to the broadcast media – mainly television – rather than the Press. Why should this be so? The explanation, I believe, lies partly in a belief that television has a greater impact than any of the other media. Then there is the fear of the unknown. While politicians have usually read the newspapers, they have often not been able to see a television programme or hear a radio programme at the time it is broadcast. Moreover whereas newspapers are expected to take a line, the broadcast media are expected to be impartial. I am also inclined to think that possibly part of the reason can be found in the direct access that MPs have to be representatives of virtually every national newspaper and most regional newspapers in the Lobby. It is true that the BBC and ITV are both represented in the Lobby, although in total on a far smaller scale than the printed media. But the tendency seems to be to pursue a grievance with a reporter, a political reporter or editor, from the newspaper concerned, perhaps at the same time attempting to influence him to write something by way of correction, or at any rate re-interpretation, rather than to seek to influence the newspaper management.

We should not, I think, be too touchy about the fact that pressures of this kind exist. They can be found in every political system where influences combine to effect results. If power is the production of intended results, influence is the climatic condition that makes the exercise of power possible. Considerations of this kind are, after all, in the heart of a free society. The habit of politicians bringing to bear what pressure they can in order to say what they want to say does not mean that journalists and broadcasters who want to say something different are on opposite sides of the barricades. The two roles have an equally respectable place in democratic theory. The politician needs to persuade in order to obtain consent, since consent is the prerequisite of achieving power and continuing to hold it. The journalist, on the other hand, owes his first loyalty to free discussion. When he stops to think about it he becomes uncomfortably aware that he has a dual responsibility as reporter and a critic, and that when exercising one of these functions he is liable to be taken to task for not living up to the other. Perhaps one of the attractions of investigative journalism is that it combines elements of both. No journalist will readily accept, indeed he will normally resent the pressures which can make his work more difficult. And yet the maintenance of a free Press, and much else besides, depends on many effective pressures from many different sources and the response to them. What is crucial is the ability of the media to withstand pressures where, after due consideration, they believe it is right to do so.

I do not regard these facts of political life as being mutually exclusive. On the contrary, I want to argue that the political and journalist roles are interdependent, with the balance between them being a matter of fundamental concern to all practitioners in the communications environment. To the politician the most important aspect of political argument is that he should win it; to the journalist the most important aspect is that the argument should take place. Thus conflicts of interest occur, it is only natural that they should do so, in the daily interaction between politicians and the media. At times tempers fray and understanding evaporates. But in the end both are on the same side. Discussion must take place. Public debate must be allowed to develop. What we understand by democracy depends on it.

I did not even in this half light detect anyone actually wince when I used the expression 'communications environment' a few moments ago. So with this passive encouragement perhaps I can move on to discuss the nature and structure of the communications environment and to identify what I believe are some of its basic elements. First there is the way in which the media are financed. The printed media have been historically dependent upon their consumers for finance, although increasingly they have come to base their finances upon advertising. The broadcast media are dependent in part upon public finance and in part upon advertising revenues. In neither case do the printed or broadcast media depend on Government favour for their money. It is true that where broadcasting is concerned Government decisions determine the amount of revenue, for example the level of the Broadcast Receiving Licence by which the BBC is financed, and the incidence of the levy on television advertising which has a direct impact on the profitability of the ITV Companies. But in neither case has there been any tendency to link political decisions on the financing of either the BBC or ITV with the content of what has been broadcast. We might take note we think, at this point, in the context of what I have just been saying about the ability, the importance of the ability to withstand political pressures, that the publicly provided element in the finances of the broadcast media has seldom if ever been threatened by the Government of the day or by the political party in power in the pursuit of particular objectives. There may at times have been an underlying fear that this ultimate deterrent might be brought into play, but I have not myself seen any evidence on either side of the fence, either working in broadcasting for quite a number of years before joining the Government in 1970 or in working in the Government since, that this uneasy awareness at the back of the corporate mind has had an impact on editorial attitudes and programme decisions. Apart from anything else, as Lord Hill of Luton pointed out shortly before the Election, there is a safeguard 'provided by what he decided as the healthy state of uncertainty with which any British Government approaches a General Election. A Government that foresees or suspects or fears a period in opposition is not going to tie the broadcasting authority too closely to its coat-tails'.

The BBC was one of the first public corporations in a deliberately created monopoly situation to emerge in twentieth century Britain. It was essentially the same concept of public finance combined with independent management which was later to come to fruition in the nationalized industries. Hand in hand with the public monopoly, and in return for the independent management, went the requirement of public accountability. Lord Crawford's Committee, which preceded the first charter of the BBC in 1927, recommended that broadcasting should be run by a public corporation 'acting as trustee for the national interest'. Those were the words used in the report of the Crawford Committee of 1927. Public accountability in this sense could have been interpreted in many ways but in practice it has been remarkably

[63]

consistent. In the broadcast media the appointment of the Chairman and Governors of the BBC and the Chairman and members of the IBA rest with the Government. Once appointed, however, from whatever background – Party politics included – it is noticeable how staunchly independent of Government the controlling bodies have been. They regard themselves, consciously and correctly, as representing the public. On occasion they make it their business to tell the Government so. Although formal accountability to Parliament exists in that the Annual Reports of the BBC and IBA have to be presented to Parliament, and can be debated in Parliament, there is not the same measure of control over either policies or expenditure that applies to the nationalized industries. And when it comes to the crucial area of the editorial content of the programmes – which after all is what broadcasting is all about – the Authorities alone are responsible. To help them in discharging their responsibilities they can turn to a proliferating network of advisory Committees – influential where educational and religious interests are concerned – but less so in the case of the mainstream of political broadcasting.

Thus it is history, or convention perhaps a better word if you like, which is the second element which makes up the communications environment. While the BBC has from the start had a specific requirement placed upon it to act as a means of information, education and entertainment (in that order) the notion of balance in the presentation of items of a broadly political character has developed in a more haphazard way. The BBC has always prized its

[64]

independence in matters of political controversy, as indeed it has over the whole field of controversy. Such independence, it has argued, has played a vital role in earning the respect of the public. From 1927 the BBC has been prevented from expressing its own opinions on current affairs or public policy and for roughly the first quarter century of its existence the Corporation operated on the basis of an interpretation of what seemed to be truthful and fair and impartial to the men of 'liberal disposition', the description used by one of them, Harman Grisewood, who determined the shape of British broadcasting in the formative years. When the change came it was more drastic and more complete than the liberally disposed had ever dreamed of. Its cause was television. The rapid expansion of BBC Television in the early 1950s was immediately followed by the introduction of Independent Television in 1955. The old leisurely conventions, such as the fourteen-day rule, which precluded the discussion of issues which were either before Parliament or likely to be debated in Parliament during the fortnight ahead, did not survive for long in the new competitive conditions. Then suddenly, while still in their infancy, both services were confronted with the most formidable political event to have faced broadcasters before or since: Suez.

In 1956, there were hardly any Ministerial broadcasts as we know them. There had been a number of broadcasts on television as well as radio by Ministers on issues of public interest, but in the main they had been confined to subjects like appeals by the Postmaster-General to post early for Christmas. Although the arrangements between the political parties and the BBC for ministerial broadcasts envisaged the possibility of the Opposition being able to reply to a controversial broadcast, in practice the exercise of a right to reply seldom arose. Normally there was no other side to the question. No one wanted to come forward and advise the public to post late for Christmas. Party broadcasts, the only programmes then as now under the complete editorial control of the political parties, carried an automatic right to reply. The Prime Minister himself appeared only on major occasions of a non-party nature, or in a rare party or Election broadcast. So when Sir Anthony Eden broadcast as Prime Minister to the nation on the Suez crisis in November of 1956 it was regarded as a declaration of public policy and as such a Ministerial broadcast in a national emergency. What he said, however, was challenged, as the policy of Anglo-French intervention on the Canal was challenged. Following prior negotiation with the broadcasting authorities the Opposition for the first time secured a right of reply the following day. Whether or not this was justified is a large question upon which many passionate hours of argument were expended. They are better left in the past. But from that moment on, nothing was the same. The elements of the new situation, post 1956 situation, arising from the relaxation of the fourteen-day rule and the exercise of the right of reply were already there embedded in BBC precedent and in practice, but they were crystalized by Suez. In a way it all must have seemed so very reasonable and fair. If difficult judgements need to be made well why not resort to a formula for their resolution? One man proposes, another opposes. Perhaps we can take some pride in the fact that politics and politicians have resolutely defied neat classifications of this sort ever since.

The benefits of these arrangements have been that Governments and Oppositions alike have had more or less equal access to the broadcast media. No one view has predominated. Other parties and interests have found it harder to break in, although once a foothold has been achieved a little tenacity will usually be enough to ensure that it is maintained. Equal opportunities to persuade, to obtain public consent for their policies have helped Opposition Parties to replace Government Parties. In this way political broadcasting has become established as a fundamental part of the political process.

The remaining elements which contribute to the communications environment are technology and sociology – the sociology of the communicators as well as the sociology of their audiences. Technological advances have been rapid; in the broadcast media exceptionally so. Colour makes television more vivid; communications satellites make possible instantaneous communication with any part of the world; the ultra high frequency wavebands make more channels available. Before long low cost video recording systems will enable people to play back programmes in their homes at times that are convenient for them. The technology of the printed media is much older and in some respects seems to be getting slower. Those who hope to obtain coverage in the London evening papers, for example, now need to be in a position to get the information out no later than noon. Technological factors of this sort have a bearing on relations between the Government and the media, but the impact is more on the machinery than on the content of communications.

There are evident similarities between people who work in the media and people who work in politics. As I have some reason to know, neither have continuity or permanence of appointment. The motivations are not all that different while educational backgrounds are increasingly similar. The newer breed of Member of Parliament could often have as easily made a career in the media, just as journalists or media executives could have set their sights on Westminster. In the new Parliament just elected fifty-eight Members gave their occupation as journalist. In politics as in the media it is tempting to draw a distinction between performance and content. The dread words 'TV personality' have no exact parallel in the press fortunately, although the stereotype is not unknown in Parliament. Verbal agility, appearance, voice, charm: these are all characteristics of the broadcast communicator which may, but need not, also be found in those who work on newspapers. The writing journalist can afford to be slower of thought, more reflective in manner, with personal appearance and voice being regarded as simply irrelevant. Differences of this sort arise I would suggest, from the nature of the media and are influenced by the time scale permitted by the technology. While television and radio enable an immediate commentary on events, in the normal course of things both the broadcast and the printed media allow much the same amount of time to be spent in preparation. When it comes to the act of communication, words typed on paper or words spoken to an electronic device, each medium calls for separate skills. Looking at the messages themselves, the printed word has the supreme advantage of permanence. The spoken word, transmitted via radio or television, is more immediate; sometimes more human; always more manifold. At the same time it suffers the disadvantage of being less reflective and less able to distinguish between groups and interests in a total audience.

It would be an error, I am sure, to spend too much time dancing on the heads of two pins labelled performance and content. In the media as in politics people have to learn to express themselves effectively, in speech and in writing. Some will have greater natural gifts than others. A reasonable level of proficiency, if not excellence, can be attained with persistence. I have no reservations at all that persuasiveness, or advocacy is a necessary part of politics, as it always has been. Nor do I believe that the advent of television has, as was once feared, led to politically irresponsible but telegenic charlatans hogging the screen. One of the virtues of the Parliamentary system is that adversaries get to know their man over a period of time. Members of Parliament, we should remember, live and work closely together for months at a time. Many of them have known each other over a long period of years. They can judge, and judge shrewdly, a Parliamentary performance. So can an experienced Lobby correspondent. It is for the commentator and the reporter in the broadcast media to help the audience to do the same when the politician arrives at the studio in the course of his business, the legitimate business of trying to persuade.

It is time now to bring the threads of my argument together. The factors going to make up the communications environment are not peculiar to the media. Some of them are reproduced in the wider political environment. Between Government and the media a relationship exists which is peculiar and precarious and which to a large extent is influenced by history, by sociology and by technology. Ambivalence pervades the relationship. Each needs the other; neither cares to admit it too often or too publicly. Both are aware that they have power; both are aware that they can only exercise it with the consent of the other. I doubt if it is possible, even if it were desirable, to lay down any principles by which the relations between the Government and the media should be conducted. The subject is too large and the ground too insecure. To do so would take us on to fundamental questions about the ways in which Government should be responsible to the community as a whole. We all know there are different answers to that question. But does the Press, I wonder, have any responsibilities towards Government as distinct from the community? Should the Press, or rather those individuals and units which make up the Press, think again and think more deeply about the underlying requirements of discussion and consent? Should Government in return accept further responsibilities towards the media, apart from its wider responsibilities towards the whole community?

These are questions which in the last resort can only be decided *in foro interno*; within the heart, mind and conscience of the individual. When contemplating subjects of this nature there is inevitably a tendency of which I am afraid I have provided another example tonight, to talk in abstractions: the media; the Government; the communications environment. Sometimes, however, in doing so we are helped to see patterns of significance which are not apparent in the course of our every day pursuits. Yet behind these abstractions, as each of us know from our own experience, communication is an act between individuals. Properly used it can be a cohesive force binding together a political society, especially at a time when the political and economic system is subject to exceptional strains. The mass media of communication can be used to inspire as well as to inform; to move towards the creation of new ideals as well as the destruction of old ones.

THE FREEDOM OF THE AMERICAN
PRESS

THE FREEDOM OF THE AMERICAN PRESS

by

KATHARINE GRAHAM

I accepted this invitation with great pleasure, but with some apprehension as well, for while this is a splendid setting for a speech, it is also humbling to be asked to join the long line of commentators who have crossed the Atlantic to report on what has come of the American experiment in self-government.

That experiment was launched three centuries ago largely by England's second sons, her dissenters and her poor. Across the generations since, most of the English commentators – from Edmund Burke to Alistair Cooke – have been somewhat ambivalent about how things in the former colonies were working out.

On the one hand, British observers have marvelled at American ideals and liberties, our ingenuity, our sense of spaciousness. On the other hand, there have been apprehensions such as those expressed by William Penn, who wrote from England in 1701:

> 'There is an excess of vanity that is apt to creep in upon the people in power in America, who . . . think nothing taller than themselves but the trees.'

Penn suggested a law requiring Americans in power to revisit England from time to time, so that – and I quote:

> '. . . They might lose themselves again amongst the crowds of so much more considerable people at the Custom-house, Exchange, and Westminster

Hall, they would ... at their return ... (he said) be much more discreet and tractable, and fit for Government. In the mean time, pray help to prevent them not to destroy themselves.'

There seems to be a similar ambivalence in commentary from Fleet Street about the American Press. In his recent book, *For Instance*, Charles Wintour, editor of the *Evening Standard*, remarked, 'An English editor must view with envy the freedom enjoyed by his American colleagues.' Harold Evans expressed similar sentiments in his thoughtful lecture here three weeks ago. But there have also been suggestions that the American press should be much more discreet and tractable because the unbridled freedom we assert can easily become a licence to distort events, destroy reputations and inflame public opinion recklessly.

For instance, Mr Evans and many of his colleagues here have praised the early Watergate reporting of *The Washington Post*. But last June in a long leading article *The* London *Times* said the moment had come for us to stop. *The Times*, in fact, accused the *Post* of conducting a 'trial by publicity' by 'publishing vast quantities of prejudicial matter' against President Nixon and thus 'making a fair trial impossible'.

Mr Nixon's partisans – who have made the same charge themselves – thought this was such an important statement that they circulated the editorial very widely at the time. As you might expect my view is somewhat different. But I agree the question is worth exploring because it illustrates the contrasts between the British and American ideas of freedom of the

Press – ideas which are grounded in two very different concepts of democratic government.

It is true that much of our coverage of the Watergate Affair would have been impossible, or at least more difficult and oblique, if the *Post* had operated under British laws.

As Mr Evans suggested, if *The Washington Post* had been *The London Post*, we would have been stopped from the start. Within hours of the break-in at the democratic national headquarters seven men had been arrested and charged. From that point on, we would have been in contempt of court for pursuing our own investigation and printing the result.

Our first lead, after all, came from entries in the address books of two of the suspects, which suggested a link between one of the defendants, Mr Hunt, and the White House. Our next big break came when a *Post* reporter, investigating the background of the defendants from Florida, established that money contributed secretly to the Nixon re-election campaign had found its way into the defendant's bank accounts. Throughout those early days, too, we were receiving tips and printing information gleaned from sources who were involved in the official investigation.

If we had been the *London Post*, we would have been in jeopardy for all of that – doubly so because we continued to pursue the matter after President Nixon had announced that his own investigation showed that the White House had not been involved – even though, as it turned out, no such investigation had been made.

We would also have run foul of the Official Secrets Act. For as the dimensions of the matter became clearer, we began to obtain more confidential accounts of the administration's cover-up. We obtained and published Government memoranda which revealed a wide variety of abuses.

As if those deterrents weren't enough, we might also have been hauled before Congress for breach of privilege. We were reporting on secret testimony which Congressional sources, among others, had leaked to us. We might also have faced legislative censure for reporting on debates and dissension within Congressional Committee and their staffs.

And, of course, if we were the *London Post* we would have run into the libel laws at every turn.

But if our Watergate reporting would have been almost impossible here, it also would have been less necessary, and that is the point. For our two countries operate under two very different forms of democratic government. Your parliamentary system has several mechanisms which we lack through which the Government can be called to account.

There is the question time in the Commons. There is the long tradition of official inquiries which have at least a reasonable chance of producing a serious result. And above all else, your government can be dissolved or forced to resign at any time. The result is that issues of compelling force can be taken to the people at once, after a campaign which seems to Americans admirably inexpensive and short. And if your Elections are sometimes inconclusive, at least they provide a formal, immediate test of public sentiment.

[78]

As we in Washington watch the Watergate scandals drag on, unresolved, it is tempting to imagine the effect that would have been produced by similar official crimes and abuses here.

We imagine how quickly a Government would have been turned out if it had engaged in 'Whitehall Horrors' a fraction as bad as the so-called 'White House Horrors' which the Nixon administration tried to suppress.

We wonder how long a British Government would have survived the revelation that No. 10 Downing Street had been secretly equipped with 'voice-activated recording devices', which I'm sure you will be interested to know are secret microphones which start recording as soon as someone begins speaking.

We wonder what would have happened here if the Prime Minister had approved a secret surveillance plan, calling for illegal burglary and wiretapping of individual citizens, and if, when that plan was frustrated by Scotland Yard's refusal to co-operate, he had set up a private Police Force to conduct such operations anyway.

What would have happened if Her Majesty's Government had conceded that illegal and unethical activities had taken place during its last campaign; what if some campaign aides and party officials had in fact pleaded guilty to illegal acts, and other former Ministers and top advisers had been indicted for such crimes as bribery, perjury, and obstruction of justice – and still others had been forced to resign under a cloud?

What would have happened if subpoenaed

evidence in a criminal case – evidence that was in the custody of the Prime Minister – turned out to have been tampered with?

Or if the Prime Minister had refused to take any questions on the scandals in the Commons for ten months, while his official spokesmen systematically deceived the public – and then conceded all his previous statements to have been – 'inoperative'? It's a wonderful new word!

Such abuses might be unthinkable here, but that is not the point. My point is that, under your system, such an affair would not have been allowed to fester so long with such severe effects on national morale and the conduct of the Government. However, qualified your faith in Parliament might be, I think you will acknowledge that at some point a Government which engaged in such practices would have been called to account and probably turned out. Certainly a British Government would not be permitted to continue to rely on a year-old electoral mandate indefinitely when such a train of abuses had been revealed and public confidence had plunged to twenty-seven per cent.

You have quick and conclusive ways to expose and deal with the sins and errors of Ministers. The burden of inquiry does not fall so heavily on the Press, and an appeal to the electorate can always be made at once if the outrage or loss of confidence is great enough.

Under our system that is not the case. The framers of our Constitution were, in the terms of their time, Republicans, not Democrats for all their faith in popular enlightenment and the ultimate rightness of public opinion. They also sought to temper the quirks and passions of the mob. Expression must be free and the Press must be unrestrained, but power is entrusted to officials for fixed terms, so that their conduct will be governed, as Hamilton wrote, by 'the deliberate sense of the Community' without 'unqualified complaisance to every sudden breeze of passion, or to every transient impulse'.

In the case of the President, a four-year term was settled on quite carefully for reasons which now sound a little quaint. That long a licence, Hamilton argued, 'will contribute to the firmness of the Executive in a sufficient degree ... (but) it is not enough to justify any alarm for the public liberty'.

Of course the founding fathers did provide for the removal of the President, other Ministers and judges by impeachment and conviction, a device borrowed from English precedents. But that was clearly meant as a drastic course, to be pursued only when the offence ... or the intractability ... was so great that the normal discipline of sustained public disaffection did not work.

When you reflect on this, as many Americans have been doing recently, it is really an extraordinary way to operate. The premium placed on public enlightenment is vast, because the guiding and controlling force – the consent of the governed – is not simply a verdict to be rendered every four years in the voting booth. Nor is it the consensus of a powerful and privileged few. It is a force and sentiment continually at play, emerging somehow from the noise and competition of free discourse and debate, protected by the first amendment and fostered by a free and independent press.

Lord Bryce, that sage observer of the American scene, remarked on this phenomenon in the American Commonwealth. 'That which ... we may call the genius of universal publicity,' he wrote, 'has some disagreeable results, but the wholesome ones are greater and more numerous ... no serious evils, no rankling sorrow on the body politic, can remain long concealed, and when disclosed, is half destroyed.'

Lord Bryce did note that this is an inefficient scheme. Public opinion in America, he said, 'is slow and clumsy in dealing with large problems ... vital decisions have usually hung fire longer than they would have been likely to do in European countries.'

This is doubly true today. Lord Bryce did not anticipate, any more than the founding fathers could, how the American executive branch would acquire such ability to dominate all the channels of expression. They did not foresee the emergence of the National Security State, cloaked in such secrecy that grave abuses of power could be concealed for years.

Even Hamilton, with his faith in a firm Executive, could not have apprehended how the Presidency would be transformed into an office of imperial bulk and perquisites, able to use the powers of the Government to reward partisans, advance special interests, squeeze political contributions from businesses, and punish and harass dissenters. Nor did most of us foresee, as recently as two years ago, how those in command of the machinery of Government could ward off inquiries, withhold evidence bearing on crimes, and throw up one roadblock after another to frustrate and delay investigations into abuses of the public trust.

Nothing illustrates better, I think, the manner in which the whole system has been cheapened and mis-used than the story of Howard Hunt and the contents of his secret White House safe. At some time prior to his involvement in the burglary of the democratic national headquarters, Mr Hunt had had made avail-able to him highly classified cable traffic, dealing with the early days of the American involvement in Viet-nam. One of his purposes in this White House authorized study was evidently to find politically in-criminating evidence against President Kennedy. He has testified that having failed to find the kind of cables he expected to, he forged some.

Those secretly forged documents, you will recall, were among the materials secretly removed from Mr Hunt's White House safe in the wake of the Water-gate arrests. Whereupon they were secretly given to a high official of Government, Mr Patrick Gray, then acting head of the FBI. Gray spirited them from the prosecutors reach in Washington to his home in Connecticut and secretly burned them with his Christmas wrappings several months later.

All of this makes publicity – the sunlight of ex-posure – doubly imperative. Unless corruption is revealed, the other checks and balances cannot be exercised. Investigations won't proceed. The Con-gress won't be roused. The courts will have no oppor-tunity to play their role. That 'deliberate sense of the community' cannot be reached unless the people have the facts.

So I come back to the essential function of the

American Press to probe, to ask the inconvenient questions, to report fully and fairly what is going on, and thus to keep the Government accountable. It is an adversary system, often more heated and contentious than we might like. And it is less efficient than it ought to be. But it's a necessary job, and one which could not be performed if the Press in America were subject to the constraints under which our colleagues here must operate.

For all of that, the problem of justice remains. Is there a point, we might ask after the facts have been exposed, at which the processes of publicity should be arrested while the agencies of justice go about their work in peace? Is there a point at which, as *The Times* argued last summer, the publication of what they called 'unsworn, untested, uncorroborated evidence' becomes so prejudicial that due process is denied and a fair trial becomes impossible?

This issue has been raised recently not only by Mr Nixon, but also by former Vice-President Agnew and some of the defendants in the Watergate criminal prosecutions now under way. Indeed, the problem of free press versus fair trial does have all the ring of a genuine constitutional dilemma, a head-on collision between two fundamental tenets of our free society.

In fact there is more sound than substance to it, I believe. While I don't propose to explore the entire problem tonight I would like to examine it as it bears on the particular cases.

First of all, consider what we are *not* talking about.

We are obviously not discussing the ordinary criminal case, the everyday assaults and robberies which clog the calendars of American courts but receive little publicity except perhaps a bare recital of the facts.

We are not talking about the average exceptional case, the kind which becomes more or less sensational because prominent people are involved, or because the offence is shocking or stirs the conscience of a community.

Such cases do suggest, I think, that pre-trial publicity does not automatically make a fair trial impossible. Look back across some of the recent American trials in which there was massive publicity not just extended coverage, but coverage of the sort which might be expected to have a prejudiced effect. Robert Kennedy's assassin, Sirhan Sirhan; George Wallace's assailant, Arthur Bremer; Angela Davis, the conspiracy trials of the Berrigans and the Chicago seven. In each case, despite all the public attention, a jury of twelve citizens was able to reach a verdict on the basis of the evidence heard in court.

There have been some cases, but very few, in which public opinion has been poisoned or the atmosphere inflamed by rash or sensational publicity. But there are time-tested remedies and safeguards which go to the inner workings of the judicial systems – to the cause of the disease, so to speak, rather than to the symptoms as they reveal themselves in press reports.

For one thing, Attorneys and public officials are entirely free to discipline themselves – so that prejudicial material does not leak to the Press at all. For instance, Judge Sirica has ordered all the Prosecutors, defendants and grand jurors involved in the

Watergate cover-up-case to refrain from discussing any aspect of the case in public.

Second, judicial procedures can be brought to bear. Jury selection has become a craft, there are elaborate procedures safeguarding the right of defendant and prosecutor to challenge biased jurors. A change of venue is a common step. Delays can be grand until tensions subside. Juries can be sequestered, as in the current case involving former Attorney-General John Mitchell and former Secretary of Commerce Mr Stans. And where publicity is found to have infected the result, a court can open a new trial – a remedy which, by the way, is far more relevant to the defendant's right of due process than finding a newspaper in contempt.

I put such stress on these alternatives because I shudder at the notion that the American Press should be restrained. That would not purify the American system of justice. On the contrary, it would tend to allow that system to be far more arbitrary and capricious than it is now. Our courts are not the British courts. The administration of justice in the United States may be less swift and sure, more over-burdened, far more open to the influences of politics and prejudice. But the surest safest way to promote due process and equal treatment under the laws is to report the ways the system does and doesn't work. Without the Press, injustices would multiply and reforms I think could not be won.

I don't pretend the Press is perfect. Errors do creep in, and some paper may occasionally embark on a crusade in blatant disregard of some person's rights. These are not light offences. But, to put it bluntly, those are the risks – the risks which freedom always bears. The costs of limiting that freedom would be higher.

All this applies with special force to what some people consider the largest or the hardest case: the matter of charges against the President or the Vice-President.

Let's look at Mr Agnew's situation first. The investigation by the United States Attorney in Baltimore was well under way at least two months before the Press got wind of it. Publication of the news alerted the country to a possibility without precedent – the possibility that an incumbent Vice-President might face a Federal indictment.

Publication also served another purpose: it insured that the investigation being conducted by members of the same administration, could not be shelved in secrecy. It insured that the charges would have to be dealt with and some kind of resolution – some kind of justice – would have to be reached, that there would be no cover-up.

Then came one of those complicated scenes which are a feature of our way of doing things. There were several weeks filled with rumours, leaks, denials, new reports, all freighted with private as well as public signals and appeals. Publicity became competitive. The investigation and the legal negotiations were going on, and at the same time all the parties – Mr Agnew and his attorneys, other figures in the case, the prosecutors, the Attorney-General, the White House – were engaged in a struggle for public sentiment. From the justice department came leaked reports that the evidence was solid; from Mr Agnew came loud complaints about smears and prejudicial news reports; from his attorneys came lots of information favourable to their case.

There were, in other words, three courts involved: the Federal Court in Baltimore; the White House; and the Court of Public Opinion. And the resolution of the matter had to be acceptable to all three, thus, finally, there was Mr Agnew's resignation, his no-contest plea to a single count of tax evasion, and the release of a forty-page bill on particulars which showed the public what the Justice Department had been prepared to charge.

In other words, all the publicity prejudiced the proceedings in only one respect: by insuring that the charges would be dealt with. It's worth noting that, despite all the leaks, the allegations which were made public during the probe were but a fraction of those alleged in the Justice Department's final list of charges. That document alleged a pattern of illegal cash payments to Mr Agnew from County, State and Federal contractors in return for favours, a pattern stretching back over many years. Much of the most damning detail was secret till the end. And it is significant, too, that for all of Mr Agnew's outraged protests about prejudicial news reports, large segments of the population and the Press apparently put more credence in his pleas of innocence until the case was disposed of and he resigned.

In Mr Nixon's case, some facts crucial to a judgement are still concealed, and no final resolution is yet in sight. But the furor is similar, though much more convoluted and prolonged. Here, too, there are three courts involved: the courts of law, the Congress, and the public opinion. There are more actors on the scene, since not only Mr Nixon but also many of his present and former associates are busily engaged in self-defence and, therefore, jousting publicly and privately over every aspect of Watergate – from the secret campaign funds and the cover-up of the burglary to the covert spying and to the matter of the President's tax returns.

There are three reasons why the charge of prejudicial publicity rings especially hollow in this case. The first is that it is such a selective charge. As made by Mr Nixon and his partisans, it is aimed only at reports which hurt his cause. They see nothing equally prejudicial in their own explanation; repeated pleas of ignorance, invocations of national necessity, attacks on the credibility of Mr Nixon's accusers, such as John Dean, and all the other arguments employed – backed by the force and prestige of the White House – in attempts to win the country to Mr Nixon's side.

The second problem is the breathtaking implications of the charge of trial by publicity, when invoked on behalf of the President of the United States. What this does, in effect, is to relieve him of the responsibilities and risks inherent in the office which he holds. It suggests that he should be regarded as an ordinary criminal suspect, for whose protection the rights of due process and a fair and speedy trial were written into the Constitution against abuses by a sovereign, not for his protection!

That Mr Nixon, as a citizen, enjoys those rights is not the point. That he, as President, should feel so threatened as to fall back on those rights appears to be an admission and a retreat more damaging than anything said against him by anyone else.

This is especially incongruous because, at the same time, Mr Nixon has been invoking in his own defence all of the powers and options which a President may command but which the common citizen cannot employ. He has, for instance, withheld evidence from the Congress and the court on the grounds of presidential privilege; he has refused subpoenas; made himself unavailable for questioning; appealed to various forums for redress; met privately with members of Congress who will be considering aspects of the case; and used all of the public relations weapons of the White House to press his cause.

This leads me to the final point: what is at stake in the Watergate crisis is not due process in the ordinary, narrow sense. To assert that is as misleading and dis-ingenuous as to argue that the only offence is a single isolated burglary. In fact, the offences involved com-prise a massive pattern of corruption and abuse – offences so serious, numerous and headstrong that they have shaken the foundation of public trust and confidence. The issue is whether and how the people and their agencies of inquiry, the Congress and the courts, can get at the entire truth, assess the damage and work out the remedies. In short, the issue – insofar as it affects the Nation's most public political figure – is due process in the broadest, most funda-mental sense.

In this context, the most prejudicial thing the Press could do would be to cease publishing and stop broadcasting some arbitrarily chosen part of what it learns. Without a free and probing Press, the events and import of Watergate would, in all probability, never have been revealed. Without that same thorough, persistent, independent Press, public debate could not proceed, the clamour and clash of opinions might never be distilled into that 'deliberate sense of the Community' which decides the matter in the end. When the American Press eases up on its vital adversary role, who is to determine how much it should ease-up, where it should stop short, what it should keep to itself – and for what purpose? Surely not the Government. Surely, in this case, not the President.

I bring you no predictions on the outcome. As I said at the beginning, I have come here to talk about the state of the great American experiment. The most that I can report with any certainty is that we are at a perilous, inconclusive point. If any lesson has emerged from the turmoil and tragedy so far, it is that the Press in America should be more free, not less. More vigorous and probing. More alert to its large responsibilities – and less easily satisfied with its own performance. For if it were, as William Penn suggested about the American people as a whole, 'more discreet and tractable', that adventure in self-government, with all its strengths and all its idiosyncracies, which is in so many ways a uniquely American experiment, might have ended years ago.

PREVIOUS GRANADA GUILDHALL LECTURES

1959
Science and Communication by Sir Edward Appleton
Television and Politics by Edward R Murrow
Dons or Crooners by Sir Eric Ashby

1960
The Language of the Gene by Professor George W Beadle
Communicating with Caliban by Professor H J Eysenck
The Human Receiving System by Lord Adrian, OM

1961
The Language of Animals by Sir James Gray
Why Scientists Talk by Professor Hermann Bondi
The Gap and the Bridge by Sir John Wolfenden

1962
The Past Speaks to the Present by Professor Yigael Yadin
Television for Teaching by Yoshinori Maeda
The Language of Economics by Dr J K Galbraith

1963
Universities and the Nation's Crisis by Professor P M S Blackett
On Making Philosophy Intelligible by Professor A J Ayer
Teaching and Machines by Professor Jerrold Zacharias

1964
Readers, Viewers, Voters by Professor Stein Rokkan
Computers, Communication and Cognition by Prof. George Miller
Man at the Centre by Professor Lord Holford

1965
ESP: What Can We Make of It by Dr J B Rhine
The Camel Driver and the Transistor by Alistair Cooke
A Humanistic Technology by Vice-Admiral H G Rickover

1966
Telecommunications – The Next Ten Years by Sir Francis McLean
From the Few to the Many by Sir Kenneth Clark
Technology and Power by Sebastian de Ferranti

public opinion. They who resort to subjects, must
be partakers of the loss. Every member of the community, must be understood, by power to re-
mand to offices to fixed or fixed that such member will be governed or function wholly by the
deliberate sense of the Community; and ought not,
qualified with bestowed on every member, either in
person, or to every member of the public.

In the case of the President — our sense is improved,
tended at appropriately carefully, so every different such
sound different shown. From a more a distinct remain—
...
Even given in a different degree... those... a given...
although, the mostly in solution, you are entitled
either.

Of course, the Republic's Counsel of... of... with the decision...
...
...
...
...
...
the decision... public... public... ...
...